SUPER FOCUS

How to Turn Your Brain into a
Laser-Sharp Concentration Machine

Kevin Garnett

© **Copyright 2020** by Kevin Garnett – All rights reserved.

In no way is it legal to reproduce, duplicate, or transmit any part of this document in either electronic means or in printed format. Recording of this publication is strictly prohibited and any storage of this document is not allowed unless with written permission from the publisher.

The information provided herein is stated to be truthful and consistent, in that any liability, in terms of inattention or otherwise, by any usage or abuse of any policies, processes, or directions contained within is the solitary and utter responsibility of the recipient reader. Under no circumstances will any legal responsibility or blame be held against the author for any reparation, damages, or monetary loss due to the information herein, either directly or indirectly.

The information herein is offered for informational purposes solely, and is universal as so. The presentation of the information is without contract or any type of guarantee assurance.

Medical Disclaimer: This book does not contain any medical advice. The ideas and suggestions contained in this book are not intended as a substitute for consulting with your doctor. All matters regarding your health require medical supervision.

Legal Disclaimer: all photos used in this book are licensed for commercial use or in the public domain. Cover image Freepik.

ERRORS

Please contact me if you find any errors.

My publisher and I have taken every effort to ensure the quality and correctness of this book. However, after going over the book draft time and again, we sometimes don't see the forest for the trees anymore.

If you notice any errors, I would really appreciate it if you could contact me directly before taking any other action. This allows me to quickly fix it.

Errors: errors@semsoli.com

REVIEWS

Reviews and feedback help improve this book and the author.

If you enjoy this book, I would greatly appreciate it if you were able to take a few moments to share your opinion and post a review online.

Table of Contents

Introduction 7

Chapter One: Focus 101 13

Chapter Two: Six Simple Ways to Improve Your Focus NOW 21

Chapter Three: The Importance of Self-Discipline and Environment 43

Chapter Four: How to Beat Procrastination 59

Chapter Five: Willpower – The Backup Asset You Need to Have 73

Chapter Six: How to Create Powerful Habits.... 81

Final Words 93

Resources 97

BONUS CHAPTER: What is Accelerated Learning? 99

Did You Like This Book? 109

Brain Teaser Answers 111

Introduction

What do you do when you wake up in the morning? Take a shower, then eat your breakfast? No! What do you do before that? You probably check Facebook notifications, see how many likes you received on your Instagram photos, skim through your emails. *Then* you take a shower and eat your breakfast. There are a dozen things distracting you. And these distractions do not end in the morning. They continue throughout the day – whether you are studying, working, spending time with friends, or even just going for a walk! Distractions are a huge part of the modern world, and as a result, *focusing* is a challenge!

But what is the point of focusing? Obviously, life cannot be lived without awareness. But you may ask yourself: *Do I really need to train my mind to develop strong focus?* What are the benefits of this?

These are fair questions. Focus, of course, extends beyond having a sense of awareness.

Developing strong focus is key to achieving success. Success is on every individual's mind. We all have an innate desire to enhance the quality of our lives. But how do we do this? We all think about the professional expertise we must obtain: improve our communication, gain an education, brush up on old skills and pick up new ones, and so forth. With all of this in mind, we overlook one particular soft skill: focus.

We all have a sense of focus, yet we need to strive to **develop strong focus**.

Developing strong focus is the precursor to mastering the professional expertise we need to find success in life. Since focus is not easily measured, we may not be completely able to comprehend or appreciate its importance, and its place in our lives. But if you take the necessary steps to develop strong focus and apply it to your tasks, you *will* notice incredible results!

Perhaps you are still a bit skeptical – and you might wonder if spending your time learning how to focus is really <u>worth</u> your time. That is a legitimate concern. But ask yourself how easily you lose focus, how easy it is for you to be distracted. Then reflect on how this affects your life.

- Do you procrastinate on your work?
- Have you sent an email without proofreading and unintentionally offended the recipient?
- Did you check your phone briefly while driving and almost get into an accident?
- Does a five-minute job take you over an hour?

The possible list is endless, and I am sure your mind is crammed with instances when losing your focus caused a detriment in your activities. Now perhaps your skepticism is assuaged. Maybe you are now concerned about your lack of focus.

Don't worry! I'm here to help. This book will teach you how to focus on the task at hand and become more productive. Distractions seem to be ever more prevalent in our modern world, but if you utilize the simple tools in this book, the distractions will not cause you to lose focus.

There are an endless number of books on how to focus, become more productive, find motivation, set goals, and so forth. This book covers all those topics and presents them in a concise manner. As opposed to pontificating about focus and all it entails, this book will serve as an instruction manual on how to develop strong focus.

This book can be referred to at any time, and you can use the steps in each chapter to practice developing strong focus. It will teach you how to develop motivation, self-discipline, and good habits, as well as how to set goals. These tricks will help you be more efficient in your daily activities and will ensure that you do not lose focus, especially in a manner that is detrimental to your success.

Some of the tools you will learn are:

- Six Simple Ways to Improve Your Focus NOW
- The Importance of Self-Discipline and Environment
- Ho to Beat Procrastination
- Willpower – the Backup Asset You Need to Have
- How to Create Powerful Habits
- And Much More!

As this book serves as an instruction manual, I would recommend you grab an empty **notebook** and keep it by your side as you are reading. At the end of each chapter will be a list of **action steps**. I would highly encourage you to complete each action item before proceeding to the next chapter.

And with all that said, let's get started: what *is* focus, exactly?

Chapter One: Focus 101

"Concentrate all your thoughts upon the work at hand. The sun's rays do not burn until brought to a focus." – **Alexander Graham Bell**

In this chapter, you will learn the basics of how to develop strong focus. These are the precursors to the more complicated methods to ensure life success!

Focus. It is a commonly used word, and in the Age of Distraction, it is probably a command that you've heard more than once. It has become increasingly challenging for us to focus on our tasks. Be it studying for an exam, completing a task for work, driving safely on the road, or even having fun, it seems that distractions are everywhere. Yet focus is a crucial aspect for living a successful life, and without it, our productivity levels will sharply decrease. In the world we inhabit, it is difficult to focus on anything. If you follow the advice in this book, it will certainly make things easier. But before we begin, we need to figure out exactly what we mean when we talk about focus.

What is Focus

Focus is **the ability to fully concentrate on one thing at a time**. It means that our attention should be on one activity – the center of interest. Perhaps the best way to illustrate its importance is to understand the perils of a *lack* of focus.

If you are cooking breakfast, a lack of focus can cause you to cook something not so edible. If you are not focused, the eggs might burn or the bacon might end up rubbery and tasteless. Oh, and don't forget about the bread – if you don't focus on how long it's been in the toaster, the toast might end up hard as a rock!

You might be thinking that burning your breakfast isn't that serious. If so, then think about this situation: You are studying for a final exam. Despite the fact that you are apprehensive, you are distracted by a noisy house, the television playing in the background, loud music emerging from your speakers, and your dog wanting your constant attention. As a result, you procrastinate on studying, and the loss of focus may have dire consequences on your exam grade!

But what about something even more serious? If you are driving a car, your focus should be on driving to your destination. Think of the distractions you come across when you are driving: other drivers, a text message, adjusting the radio station, enjoying the scenery. With these distractions, it can be easy to lose focus on the center of interest – the driving itself. This loss of focus can be dangerous! A simple lack of focus, whether you look at a notification on your phone for a few seconds or are daydreaming endlessly, can cause a tragic accident on the road.

As you read this book, you will learn about different distractions that affect your focus. Not all of them may seem obvious, but if you take a moment to reflect, you will realize that your lack of productivity, piling too much on your plate, procrastination, will all negatively affect your ability to concentrate.

The point of this book is to help you develop strong focus.

As Sharp as A Laser!

You've probably heard the term "laser-sharp focus" before. Let's be honest, it sounds like an unnecessarily fancy phrase! In reality, it simply means being able to pinpoint your focus (like a laser) onto one task at a time. Your life will be inundated with tasks, and a laser-sharp focus allows you to tackle them by breaking them down into steps and then focusing on each step individually. To develop a laser-sharp focus and therefore find success in life, you must master self-discipline, increase your productivity, find motivation, augment your willpower, set goals, and follow a set of good habits.

Before you embark upon exploring these areas, pull out your notebook and attempt this short activity:

- **Write down your life's purpose or mission statement.** Do not worry about being grand; something as simple as "I wish to be happy and live a stress-free life," is sufficient!
- **Write down the following skills and grade yourself** for each one on a scale of 1 to 10, with ten being highly adept: Self-Discipline, Motivation, Willpower, Setting Goals, and Productivity.
- **Write a short paragraph on how well or how badly you focus.** Here is an example: *I live with a sense of awareness. I do not text*

and drive or do anything irresponsible like that. However, generally, I do have difficulty focusing on one thing at a time. When I am cooking, I am also checking my phone. If I am working on the computer, I often aimlessly browse the Internet and therefore postpone my work. I do procrastinate when I have a task that does not have an immediate deadline.

Refer to this page in your notebook as a constant reminder that you acknowledge your strengths and weaknesses, and what you would like to improve upon. As you read this book, you will learn about the different skills to improve upon. At any time, if you feel that you have improved upon the skills, change the grade for that skill. So, if you were originally a 3 on self-discipline and you feel that your self-discipline has improved, change the number to whichever number you now feel is appropriate.

Now let's jump right into the first topic! I am sure you are eager to learn the methods for developing strong focus, but first, we must have a look at the basics.

Chapter Two: Six Simple Ways to Improve Your Focus NOW

"How we spend our days is, of course, how we spend our lives." – **Annie Dillard**

Alice is doing groceries in the supermarket when she bumps into John. *"Hi Alice, how are you?"*, says John. Alice:*"Oh I'm fine, thanks!"*. John: "And how's your son Jimmy? Is he still unemployed?". "Yes, he is," Alice replies, *"But he is meditating now."* John: "Meditating? What's that?"
Alice: "*I don't know. But it's better than sitting around and doing nothing!"*

Okay, I admit it: that was a bad joke!

But as it turns out, meditation offers a lot more than just sitting and doing nothing. As a matter of fact, it one of the best things you can do if you want to increase your power of concentration.

Focusing is not as simple as it might seem – particularly with the distractions of the modern era. However, with the five strategies set out in this chapter, you'll be able to become a master at focus.

As you read along, make note of these tactics and try them out. Perhaps design a schedule of what focus activities you can complete each day. I would tell you to put the book down and try an activity out, but let's focus on one thing at a time!

Meditation

If there is one thing you take away from this book, let it be this: where many productivity strategies fail to stand the test of time, meditation has been proved in study after study to increase the strength of one's focus.

What is meditation? At its core, it's a practice where you continually return your focus to a single object of attention. The most common object of concentration is the breath. However, it can also be a word you repeat (mantra), a visualization, your body, music, et cetera.

Each time you notice your mind wanders, you return the spotlight of your mind to the focus of your attention. This practice strengthens your attention muscle more than any other practice or technique.

In one meditation study, the subjects participated in two 45-minute guided meditation per week. They were also asked to meditate at home. The researchers found that, after only a few weeks, the working memory capacity of the meditators had increased by more than 30%! The participants in the control group did not show this kind of improvement.

Moreover, various studies have shown that meditation can increase willpower, enhance creativity and improve your sleep (which is a big one, if you want to be more focused).

One study even showed that eight weeks of daily meditation practice increased gray matter in the brain. So, meditation actually changes the structure of your brain!

Meditation is not as complex as it appears and need not be a lengthy process.

If you are a beginner in the meditation practice, I recommend that you start with focusing on the breath. The breath is always there, so it's an easy object of attention.

Let's try it out now. Are you in? We are going to take one conscious breath. One inhalation, and one exhalation. Don't change your breath, simply observe it, going in and out.

Ready? Please put this book down for a second, and...go!

If you have never meditated before: Congratulations! You have just set your first step on the meditation path.

So, how do you build an actual meditation practice?

Here is what you have to do:

- **Set a timer for yourself.** You can meditate any time of the day, but perhaps you should do it early in the morning before having to begin the tasks of the day. You can start with just a few minutes, and build up over time.
- **Sit in a comfortable position.** You can choose to sit cross legged, with or without a cushion. It is also perfectly fine if you sit on a chair. In meditation, it is not about how you look, but about what's happening inside. If you are sitting cross legged, but you are

experiencing discomfort from the very beginning, don't meditate in that position. Just don't do it. You can always choose to work on your flexibility so you can sit cross legged in future meditations, but for now accept the limits of your body. Whether you sit cross legged or on a chair, in both cases it is crucial that you sit up straight. Here's

- **Close your eyes.** Also make sure that you are in silence – turn off any background noises. Put your phone on silent, except for the timer option if you are using it as a timer.
- **Focus on the breath coming in and going out.** It is imperative that you do not allow yourself to be distracted by other things: do not think about when the timer will go off; do not think of everything that needs to be accomplished for that day. Your focus should be solely on the image you created.
- **Don't judge yourself if you get distracted.** Think of the mind as a puppy. If you have a puppy in your kitchen, it's going to

run around, it's going to pee in a corner. But you wouldn't get upset. Instead, you would look at it, smile and think: *"It's just a puppy, it doesn't know any better."* An untrained and unfocused mind is like that puppy. It will learn with practice. If it wanders, don't get upset: simply smile and notice that it is a puppy now, but it will learn, eventually!

- **Take a moment to come back.** When you finish meditating, don't immediately get up. Allow yourself to come back by staying with your eyes closed for a while and observe the effects of your meditation practice

Reading

Reading is another wonderful activity for training yourself to focus. Unlike listening to music or watching a film or television show, reading is an active form of entertainment. The ideas and messages of the author are overtly passed on to the reader, and the reader must use his or her

imagination and understanding to comprehend the text. Reading has become one of the most difficult pastimes to enjoy, and it due to a lack of focus that we become distracted more easily. But, without our realizing, we are looking at text constantly:
- glancing at the news app on our phones
- a sign on the street
- an advertisement in a magazine, or
- the endless text messages we receive on a daily basis

Reading has not gone out of fashion! However, this fast-paced style of reading does not do much in helping us train our minds to focus. That is why reading a long block of text is the best method.

Set a time during your day to read uninterrupted. As with meditation, this need not be long. Perhaps aim for thirty minutes of reading. Alternatives could be to read an entire newspaper or magazine article; or one chapter of a novel; or a certain number of pages per day. With reading, as with meditation, silence is important – if you can get it. See if you can read early in the morning or late at night while everyone in your house (if there are others) is still asleep. If you would like to read during your lunch break at work, see if there is a quiet space in the office. And, of course, if there is a library within your reach, that is the best location for quiet reading. Ensure that you are actively reading: your eyes should be on the text. Your phone should be on silent, and if you are particularly addicted to it, turn it off. The concentration needed for reading will train you to focus on one activity at a time for a prolonged duration.

Create a Daily To-Do List

One of the most important, yet most overlooked, aspects of training yourself to focus is to organize your tasks – or in simpler terms, to create a to-do list. Often, we may be tempted to "go with the flow," but for a busy person in the modern world, organizing your activities and tasks is a necessity.

Start simple by writing your tasks for the day on a sheet of paper.

Make it a ritual to write these tasks the night before. List them in the order in which they should be completed – with high priority tasks or tasks that need immediate attention first. Here is a sample of what can be written:

<u>TO-DO LIST</u>

- Cook breakfast (task which needs immediate attention).
- Call the plumber to fix the leak in the bathroom (task which needs immediate attention/high priority).
- After calling, read the headline article in today's newspaper in its entirety.
- Head to work!
- During lunch break, put phone away and focus on eating.
- Upon arriving home, take out the trash.

- Study for exam.
- Cook dinner.
- After dinner, spend 30 minutes on hobby.
- Meditate for twenty minutes.

The above should give you an idea of what a typical to-do list may look like. You may fill in as you deem necessary. This may seem unnecessary at first, but you will notice that if you do not organize your day, you may forget to complete a crucial task such as calling the plumber (and therefore dealing with a leak for a few more days) or taking out the trash (and having it smell up your entire house).

As with the example to-do list, write down your necessary tasks for the day and organize them by priority. The tasks with the highest priority should be listed at the top of the page, and the tasks with the least sense of urgency should be at the bottom. Sometimes, it may be difficult to figure out the priority of a task. Here is what you can ask yourself to figure it out:

- What is the deadline of this task?
- What is the worst-case scenario if this task is not completed by this time?
- How will I benefit from completing this task ahead of my other tasks?
- Can this task be completed at any time?

So, here are two sample tasks: going for a daily run and studying for your math exam.

Let's begin with tackling the task of going for a daily run.

- There is no deadline. However, I would like the run to be completed today. I do not wish for this to be postponed.
- If I postpone my run, it can develop into a habit and I may completely break the routine of my daily run.
- This is a great form of exercise and will make me feel energetic for the rest of the day.

- Yes, but if I do it in the morning, I will feel energized for the remainder of the day. My gym may be closed at night, so I might have to run outdoors at night and/or it might be too dark to run at night!

Now let's have a look at the second task: studying for your math exam.

- The exam is three days away and is quite tough, so I need to study every day until exam day.
- If I postpone my studying, I will probably not fare well on the exam.
- I will be more prepared for the exam, and more relaxed about taking it.
- Yes, but since it is difficult, I should study each day for a set amount of time.

Now what do you think? Both are important tasks. The run does not have a deadline, but it is needed to prepare yourself for the day. The math exam is around the corner, and due to its difficulty, studying each day is imperative.

It is best to run first thing in the morning, as you may not be able to visit the gym in the evening or run outside in the dark. The early morning run will provide you with energy for the day. Then you can study for your exam. The time of day you study is not important as long as you are able to study each day, and for a sufficient duration.

Do the Most Difficult Task First

Creating a to-do list gives your day structure. If you want to supercharge your day, though, here's a real game changer: <u>begin with the most difficult task</u>. Every to-do list has easy, enjoyable tasks *and* difficult, boring tasks. Most people prefer to do the fun tasks first. Yet, as they procrastinate on the challenging tasks, those same tasks take up headspace. It's that nagging voice in the back of your mind that tells you you should really do your taxes, call that client or edit that document. The effect is twofold:

- **You're focus is scattered**: it shifts between the task you're working on, and the guilt and pressure you feel about the needs-to-be-done task you're *not* working on.
- **You're less productive**: scattered attention takes up a lot of energy. Moreover, you're wasting energy on thinking and worrying about the task you don't like to. While the task doesn't get done! At the end of the day, you're not getting done as much as you could.

The way to tackle this is to take a look at all the tasks on your to-do list for the day and start with the one you dislike the most. That's right, that task you really don't feel like doing! This is known as 'eating the frog', a term coined by Mark Twain. He once said that if eating a frog is the very first thing you do in the morning, you'll be able to go about your day with the satisfaction of knowing that that is most likely the worst thing that is going to happen to you all day long.

From personal experience, I can tell you that eating the frog is amazing! Sure, it doesn't take the task any more fun. But often I find that when I'm actually doing the task, it's not as bad or difficult as I thought it would be. Also, it often takes less time than I thought it would. The best thing is when it's done. Imagine having finished the most difficult task of the day by 10am. You still have your whole day ahead of you! And with that challenging task no longer weighing on your shoulder, no longer taking up headspace, the rest of the to-do list just feels so light...

Work in Uninterrupted Time Blocks

Another way to double your focus is to work in uninterrupted blocks of time. This is something Cal Newport recommends in his popular book *Deep Work*. Although we all have the same 24 hours in a day, we have control over how we spend those hours. Two different people can sit behind a desk for five hours, yet one of those two can get way more done than the other. The reason? That person works *smart*.

Here's how you can work smart, too. Schedule a few 60-90 minute blocks per day for work that requires your full, focused attention. That stuff that really makes a difference. If you're familiar with the 80/20 rule: the 20% of the tasks that result in 80% of your results. Use a timer and make sure you won't be interrupted. That means: a quiet room, with the door closed. Also, turn off email and phone notifications. You could even go as far as turning off your Wi-Fi. If you need internet access for the task, use a website blocker app to block access to all your favorite procrastination sites.

Try it out for a week; I promise, you'll thank me later!

Tease Your Brain!

Strengthening your focus should not feel like a tedious undertaking. A fun way of training the power of your mind are brain teasers.

Brain teasers improve your memory and memorizing is an aspect of developing strong focus. There are several methods to attempt to develop strong focus by teasing your brain.

Here are a few brain teasers that will mess with your head:

1. **Brain Teaser 1**: Rearrange the letters in NEW DOOR to make one word.
2. **Brain Teaser 2**: What occurs twice in a moment, once every minute, yet never in a billion years?
3. **Brain Teaser 3**: At opposite ends are my mouth and my head. I run for miles without leaving my bed. What am I?

See 'Brain Teaser Answers' at the end of this book for the correct answers!

You can also do brain teasing in combination with reading, one of the other recommend ways to train your concentration muscle. Here are a few suggestions:

- As you are reading, count the frequency of a particular word in a paragraph. To really challenge yourself, count the frequency of a particular letter in a paragraph.
- After finishing a chapter or an article, write or speak out loud a brief summary of what you read.
- Teach what you have read to another person. In as much detail as possible, outline the key points of what you read so that the other person can have a clear understanding without having to read the text themselves.

This only scratches the surface of the fun you can have with brain teasers. Do a bit of research to see what works best for you. Things like trivia games, learning a musical instrument, or even completing a jigsaw puzzle are all methods to tease your brain.

Action Steps

Before we move on, ensure that you implement these steps in your routine:

- Meditate for five minutes per day. Set a fixed time each day during which you will meditate. This can change later, but for at least a week, aim to meditate at the fixed time.
- Pick up a book. Read a chapter or a certain number of pages per day. If you are subscribed to a newspaper or magazine, aim to read one article per day. Again, set a fixed time to read your material, and for at least a week, aim to read at the fixed time.

- Write down the ten most important tasks for the week. Prioritize them in descending order, with the highest priority at the top, and the lowest priority at the bottom. Cross off the tasks as you complete them.
- Every day, start with the most difficult or boring task.
- Search for brain teasers online. Try to do at least one per day, for a week.

You now know what focus is, as well as six ways to strengthen your ability to concentrate. These steps will help you develop discipline and make it easier for you to focus and prioritize your tasks.

In the next chapter, you will learn about how you can use your increased focus to be more productive. Also, you'll gain a better understanding of how your environment impacts your ability to focus.

Notes

In one meditation study... Dianna Quach et al., "A Randomized Controlled Trial Examining the Effect of Mindfulness Meditation on Working Memory Capacity in Adolescents," Journal of Adolescent Health 58, no. 5 (2016): 489–96.

One study even showed that... Luders, E., A. W. Toga, N. Lepore, and C. Gaser. "The Underlying Anatomical Correlates of Long-Term Meditation: Larger Hippocampal and Frontal Volumes of Gray Matter

Chapter Three: The Importance of Self-Discipline and Environment

"Your input shapes your output." – **Zig Ziglar**

In this chapter, you will learn the importance of self-discipline, environment and your state of mind to build your focus and boost your productivity.

Hyper Focus Doubles Your Productivity

Perhaps the most significant result of supercharged focus is increased productivity. Being able to get things done has become a challenge. Focus becomes crucial in our daily lives in order for us to become more productive. The necessity of productivity ranges from our careers, to our studies, to our chores. Before we go on, take a moment to reflect on how productive you are. Ask yourself the following questions:

- Do you often finish your work at the last minute?
- Have you ever submitted work long before a deadline?
- How much progress do you make each day per task?

Maybe you picked up this book because you know that you're slacking with regard to all three. You finish your work at the last minute, never submitting it before the deadline; as a result, you are always under pressure to finish your work on time. As for progress, are you able to quantify your work so far? If you are to write 6,000 words in a span of three days, and have only written 500 words on the first day, was this a productive day? Focus is needed to improve your productivity.

Self-Discipline: The Secret Ingredient to Boosting Your Productivity

To achieve your long-term goals, you need to be work on them consistently. That requires not only focus, but also discipline. The word itself echoes a strict regimen, and we may wish to shy away from it. But discipline and developing strong focus go hand-in-hand. *Self*-discipline is more of a challenge, but it is an even greater technique for improving your focus.

What is the difference between discipline and self-discipline?

Discipline is thrust upon you and forces you to focus. If you are given an exam and have an hour to complete it, you will be able to focus on the exam and give your best effort. But what about self-discipline? If you decide to write a blog post but no outside force imposes a deadline on you, you must assign a deadline to yourself. The ultimate test of self-discipline is if you finish your blog post by your own deadline. Self-discipline is a byproduct of self-motivation. Enjoying the process and the journey to achieving your goals becomes of the utmost importance. Setting small, achievable goals is the key to success.

Having a well-thought out routine is the preliminary step to self-discipline. Let's go back to the example of writing and publishing a blog post. Think of the routine you would need to develop to accomplish this goal. How many words is the blog post? When do you wish for the post to be published?

Let's say it's 500 words and is to be published within five days. Your routine could consist of writing 100 words per day. If you stick to this routine, it will improve your self-discipline.

Let's do a bit of practice to improve your self-discipline:

- Write down one simple task that will not take much of your time.
- Write down the routines you will follow to complete this task. The best format is to list the routines in the order they need to be completed – the first step, followed by the second step, and so forth.
- At the end of each day, write down if you followed the routines. Check off the routines as you complete them.

If you develop this habit of following routines, it will improve your self-discipline. Once you have developed self-discipline, you will have completed a major step in developing strong focus!

If you would like to learn more about how can gain more self-control, you may want to check out my book *'Self-Discipline 101. Get Things Done By*

Learning How To Use Habits, Routines and Mental Toughness to Achieve Your Goals.'

Know Your Why

The Internet is full of motivational quotes and images. Yet motivating oneself is a challenge, and a lack of motivation is correlated to a lack of focus. To improve our focus, we must first develop a motivation to achieve something. If we are not motivated to achieve, we become lethargic – and lethargy is the enemy of focus. To develop motivation, we must first have an end goal. You need to know your <u>*why*</u>.

I am sure you have wanted something before in your life. But there have been times that despite you wanting something, you did not follow through or you did not take all the necessary steps to attain what you wanted. You must approach what you *want* as if it is a *need*. If something is a need, then you commit yourself to it because needing something leads to a sense of self-discipline, which will help you achieve your goals. When one needs something, there is a strong sense of focus toward achieving the goal.

Self-discipline starts with changing your attitude toward your goal – change your wants to needs. Treat your hobby as if it is on the same level as your career. You have decided to take your fate in your own hands with no one and nothing to blame except your own effort – or lack thereof.

Commitment toward one's goals requires perseverance, hard work, getting up each time you are knocked down, assessing your weaknesses, and working to overcome them at all costs.

When you commit to a goal, there is no room for hopelessness or despair. You must have the self-discipline to achieve your goals. It is imperative to see the bigger picture, and a razor-sharp focus at each small step which will help you achieve your goal.

Setting goals can be a frightening endeavor. But setting goals is the precursor to developing strong focus. With nothing in sight, there is nothing for us to focus on. Take a pause and write down one goal in these three categories:

- **Profession or Education** – What would you like to achieve in your career or desired career? A promotion? Maybe securing your dream job? If you choose education, do you wish to gain admission to a particular academic institution? Do you want to ensure you get the highest grade possible on an upcoming exam?
- **Personal** – This is a broad subject, but think of a goal you wish to accomplish in your personal life. Do you wish to gain or lose weight – set a particular number of pounds that you wish to gain or lose. Or perhaps you

are afraid of public speaking, and wish to boost your confidence?
- **Leisure** - What is one leisurely pursuit that you wish to attain? Do you wish to travel to Brazil? Make a note! Want to take up acting? Make a note!

How Your Environment Influences You

If you believe you are strong-willed individual who acts independently of your surroundings, I hate to break it to you: you are mistaken.

In his book *'Willpower Doesn't Work'*, Benjamin Hardy even goes as far as to say: *"You are who you are because of your environment. Want to change? Then change your environment."*

So, am I saying that people are a *victim* of your surroundings?

No, certainly not! Instead, understanding the effect of your environment gives you real power: instead of relying on willpower (which is a depletable resource), you can now create an environment that is conducive to being productive and achieving your goals.

For many readers, this may be the most challenging aspect of being able to develop strong focus. Right now, your environment may not be conducive to helping you accomplishing your goals. Your environment may not be conducive to developing strong focus. But don't fret: there are ways around this!

First, identify what you dislike about your environment. What is it about your surroundings that hinders you from focusing? By now, you should know what I am going to suggest you do. Make a list! After you make a list of the issues, you can begin listing solutions for them.

Perhaps you need silence to complete your work. Your home is noisy; worse, you live on a busy street. Find a library to study. Maybe even invest in a pair of noise-cancelling headphones. Or, find a particular time to complete your work. Is the house quiet early in the morning or late at night? If so, schedule time during those early or late hours to complete your work.

Also ask yourself: are the people I spend a lot of time with pushing me forward, or dragging me down? It was Jim Rohn who, famously, said: *"You are the average of the five people you spend the most time with."* I personally really live by this rule; I'm very picky about who I allow in my inner circle.

Watch Your State of Mind

Focus, self-discipline and a positive environment can only really boost your productivity if your heart is in it. If you doubt yourself, you're sabotaging your own progress. Similarly, if you aren't handling stress well, you'll lack motivation and energy to keep hustling.

Luckily, handling stress is not as strenuous as it sounds. Here are two simple ways that alleviate stress immediately:

- **Be positive**! These days we are inundated with messages to be positive. Now, I will not tell you that you need to be positive at all times. Absolutely not! But being negative, pessimistic, or cynical is deterring your focus. If you are cynical about whether or not you will receive top marks on your exam, do you think you will be able to focus properly during your study time?
- **Work on your health**. I'm probably kicking in an open door with this one, but I want to emphasize it regardless. Your health will affect your ability (or lack thereof) to focus. You do not need to become a fitness buff, but exercising one's body and mind (more about

this later) and maintaining a healthy diet will declutter your internal environment. Think of it this way: you can buy a Ferrari, but you won't get very far if you fill it up with swamp water instead of gasoline!

Action Steps

Take the following action steps, and take notes in your notebook:

- Write down any issues you have with productivity. BE SPECIFIC! Do you not complete your work on time, or do you complete it just before a deadline? How much of your day is spent on completing your tasks and how much is spent procrastinating?
- What about self-discipline? Must someone else impose discipline on you? Are you able to set your own deadlines and routines and stick to them?
- Take a pen and a piece of paper, and spend 30 minutes to come up with your *why*. Why do you want to improve your focus? What goals would you like to achieve that require a stronger ability to concentrate for a long stretch of time?

- Think about ways in which you can improve your environment. What can you remove that distracts you? What could you bring into your environment that would help you be more productive?
- How would you rate your state of mind? Do you believe in yourself, and your ability to achieve your goals? How are your energy levels? Could you change something in your diet that could help improve your ability to focus?

In the next chapter, we will discuss the #1 enemy of productivity: procrastination.

Read it *now*. Don't put it off!

Chapter Four: How to Beat Procrastination

"My own behavior baffles me. For I find myself doing what I really hate, and not doing what I really want to do!" – **St. Paul** (Romans 7:15)

They say the road to hell is paved with good intentions. The same can happen if you don't follow through on your intention to improve your focus and consistently do the tasks that need to be done to achieve your goals.

To be productive means keeping the urge to procrastinate under control. One of the best explanations of how a procrastinator's mind works comes from Tim Urban, the author of the popular Wait But Why blog. He points out that there is not only a 'rational decision maker' in our brain, but also an 'instant gratification monkey'. And they don't get along well...I highly recommend you check out his TED talk 'Inside the mind of a master procrastinator'!

In this chapter, you will learn about procrastination – and how to fight it! You will also learn to put aside multitasking and focus on one thing at a time.

Focusing is not as simple as it sounds! It takes energy and dedication to develop self-discipline, stay motivated, to create an ideal environment – all of which are necessary to develop strong focus! With every step of the way, the urge to procrastinate is trying to take over control...

Procrastination can come at us in different ways. The most obvious way is where you just don't *feel* like doing what you should be doing. Netflix is just so much more fun! The second way is where you are working hard, but put too much on your plate, resulting in feeling overwhelmed. That can lead to a system shutdown, and before you know it, you're watching cat videos on YouTube for 5 hours, while stuffing yourself with Pringles...

Let's take a look at how you can tackle these potential pitfalls.

"I'll Get To It Later!"

Procrastination is a huge issue in the modern world. It is also one of the greatest impediments to developing strong focus. If you recall the example of writing a blog post in the last Chapter, I wrote about having to complete a portion of the blog post each day in order to complete the blog post by your set deadline. I suggested writing 100 words per day in order to complete a 500-word blog post within five days. But what if you write 50 words on the first day, and tell yourself that you'll make up for it the following day? What if you lose an entire day of work due to your lack of focus? Procrastination is the antithesis of focus, and here is how to stamp it out:

- Make a list of at least three things that distract you from your work. Do you check your phone constantly? Are you always on social media? Does listening to music disturb your workflow?
- Time your work. While you do not have to think of it as improving your marathon score, see how much time it takes you to do the same amount of work. Does writing 100 words take half an hour on one day and an entire hour the next day? Of course, there's nothing wrong if your work differs a bit, but for any routine tasks, see if your times are vastly different at different times.
- Time your time-wasting! At the end of the day, add up the minutes and see how much time you were occupied with activities that are not productive. If they are taking a significant

portion of your time, you know that your procrastination needs looking into!

Let's look at your results and what to do about them:

You need to lower the occurrence of, or if possible, eliminate the three things that distract you from work. If you check your phone constantly, then turn it off while you work. If this is not an option, keep it out of sight – but not in your pocket! Keep it in a drawer or even on a shelf or platform which you cannot easily reach. What about social media? If you receive mobile notifications from your social media platforms – turn them off!

Better yet, delete the apps from the phone so you can only check social media through your computer. After using social media, log out of the platform – so if you wanted to access the platform again, you would have to go through the additional step of logging in.

Let's say it took you twice the amount of time to complete the same amount of work from one day to the next! Why? Was there an emergency distraction? Or more likely, did you procrastinate? As I stated, you do not need to think of it as running a marathon, but try to remain within a certain range. If it took you 30 minutes to complete a task on the first day, the time it takes should not exceed 40 minutes the next day. Put yourself under pressure to complete your work within this time range.

This ties in to the responses for Step 1. How long are you scrolling through your phone and not making an important call or responding to an important text? Are you playing a game that you will never win, opening an app you never use, or attempting to take the perfect selfie which you will never take? Once you have recorded the time spent on these activities, gradually try to decrease the time. Ideally, you will eliminate them entirely, but as a start, see if you can spend five minutes playing the game as opposed to your recorded 15 minutes.

"I'll Do It All At Once!"

Have you ever gone to a restaurant and after ordering a delicious-sounding meal, realized that you will not finish all the food? Have you ever realized that there is literally too much on your plate? You may feel the same way about your day-to-day life: be it your work, studying, familial responsibilities, chores, or social life. Now, most likely, this will not change, as life will continue to be busy. However, maybe you are taking on too many things at once and are therefore unable to focus on anything. Have you ever heard of a jack of all-trades, master of none? They have not mastered anything because there is not a single trade on which they have focused all their attention!

To illustrate this, let me share with you an example from my own life. I'm very curious and get easily excited about new things. This is a double-edged sword. It makes my life fun, yet it can also cause feeling overwhelmed. Many years ago, I went on a holiday to Italy. I fell in love with the food and the country, and decided I wanted to learn the Italian language. Back home, I enrolled in an Italian language course. But it didn't take long before I was behind on my homework and my motivation started to plummet. I dropped out after about six classes. The reason? I was working an 80-hour corporate job. When I finally had some time to unwind and recharge, I didn't feel like doing my homework. What also didn't help was that I didn't have a strong 'why'. The decision to study Italian had been an impulsive one and was only based on a holiday trip. Now that the shine was wearing off, I just wanted to chill on a Sunday.

Multi-tasking is not inherently a bad thing. However, it can be detrimental to your work. Until you have mastered multi-tasking, it is better to focus on one task at a time. The previously discussed process of organizing your day will be crucial in organizing your tasks. It will allow you to complete all your tasks by their due dates, while being able to work on each task one at a time and giving each task your best effort.

This can be accomplished by scheduling and timing. Schedule your tasks so that you work on things one at a time. Often, we are answering an email while studying for an exam, as well as preparing that balance sheet for work, and doing push-ups in between so you can stay fit! For now, concentrate on improving your focus by taking on one task at a time. You will recall creating a to-do list and organizing your tasks; now you will go further and set timings for each task. Organize your tasks from highest priority to lowest priority. Now, as an extra step – add the deadline when this task should be completed.

Let's say we have a friend named Bob. Here is an example of his list of tasks:

- Prepare report for work (due in three days)
- Write essay for history class (due in five days)
- Answer emails to clients (due in a week)
- Go for a run (complete by end of day)
- Wash the car (complete by end of day)

You will notice that tasks 4 and 5 are to be finished today, yet they are at the bottom of the list. This is because Bob feels that the first three tasks can be worked on simultaneously. He does exactly this – cycling between his report, his essay, and his emails. But due to this multitasking, he lacks focus and his report and essay are subpar, and his emails are not proofread.

Here is a better idea of what Bob should do: He should go for his run first thing in the morning. This will energize him for the day. After his run, he should immediately wash his car. Most likely, he will sweat during his run and will wish to take a shower afterward. However, after showering, he would not wish to undergo the laborious task of having to wash his car!

Once these two tasks are completed, he has the rest of the day to work on the remaining three. While they all have different deadlines, it is most likely that Bob needs to complete a small portion of each task each day, as they are arduous tasks, which is why he has been multitasking.

So, let's look at these three remaining tasks in meticulous detail. Bob's report is to be nine pages long. His history class essay is to be 3,000 words. And he has 14 emails to send to clients in a week's time. This is a lot of work, so Bob has to complete a portion each day. Here is how he could break it down to focus on each task one at a time:

- Complete three pages per day on the report.
- Write 600 words per day for his history class essay.
- Write two emails per day to clients.

As for the order, this is up to Bob. He could benefit from working on the most difficult task first or completing the easier tasks first to then focus on the harder tasks. Bob – and you – should try out both methods to see what works better.

Action Steps

Let's recap: what have we learned?

Procrastination is harming your ability to develop strong focus, and while multitasking is no crime, it is just as responsible as procrastination in causing you to have weak focus. You need to identify these two facets as issues, and work on resolving them.

Here is what to do before moving on to the next chapter:

- Identify the things you do which cause you to procrastinate on the important tasks. Detail these distractions by recording how much time you spend on each one.
- Use a timer to track how long you work on a task. Are you working efficiently? In the future, do you think you could spend less time to complete that same task?
- Prioritize and set goals for completing your tasks, either in full or in portions, in order.

- Work on one task at a time.

In the next chapter, you will learn about understanding trade-offs and how this ties in to improving your willpower.

Chapter Five: Willpower – The Backup Asset You Need to Have

"Do or do not do. There is no try." – **Master Yoda**

Up until now, we have spoken about how you can develop your focus, use self-discipline and shape your environment to increase your productivity and beat procrastination.

If you do all these things right, there isn't much need to rely on willpower. Studies have shown that willpower is like a muscle that can be depleted. Relying solely on willpower would be a very shaky foundation for any goal you are trying to achieve.

Yet, willpower is a wonderful complementary asset to have. In this chapter, you will learn the importance of willpower in making decisions.

The Bigger Picture

In her book '*The Willpower Instinct*', Kelly McGonigal defines willpower as the ability to control your attention, emotions, and desires. You may think that we have already discussed motivation and self-discipline, so why the need to discuss willpower? Are these two concepts not the same? Is the information redundant? Not really.

Willpower *is* certainly the product of both motivation and self-discipline, but it goes a step further. Willpower requires focusing on the bigger picture, or on the destination – not worrying about the tension during the journey. So far, I have told you how certain activities improve your focus as well as how improving your focus helps with certain facets of life. Reading attentively improves focus;

improving focus increases productivity. When it comes to willpower, you will need a strong sense of focus. And having willpower will improve your sense of focus.

Let us go back to the example of writing a blog post and completing it by a deadline, as a means to improving your self-discipline. You have managed to publish your blog post within the five days you set, and you stuck to the routine of writing 100 words per day. But a month has passed, and no one has read your blog post. It does not seem to garner interest. Perhaps this does not discourage you immediately (good for you!), but in the long run, if the results do not show after immense work, you may be susceptible to losing motivation. Your self-discipline will dwindle; and there is now an urgent need for willpower.

What is the bigger picture in this situation? The bigger picture is that you are growing your blog; you are building your writing portfolio, which will lead to your dream career as a writer! But this lack of response from a potential audience is hindering you. More and more you focus on giving up rather than on persevering! To alleviate this issue, here is what you should focus on:

- **What is the bigger picture**? It is not a response to your most recent task. It is what it will lead to. Think of the bigger prize at the end. Taking a public speaking course may not yield immediate results – but in the long run, this may impress an interviewer and land you your dream job!
- **Measure your progress toward your long-term goal**. So, if the goal is to lose 10 pounds, do not fret if your weight remains the same after one hour on the treadmill. Weigh yourself after a month of consistent exercising and see how much progress you have made.
- **Focus on the essentials**. What needs to be achieved now? This does not mean to forgo all your goals; rather, it means focusing on the

necessary, immediate goals. You want to save $1,000. You also want to complete your degree with top grades. And you want to visit the new planetarium as soon as you can. Since you have learned about prioritizing, look at your goals and see what needs to be done immediately and focus on achieving that goal first. You may need to save the $1,000 to pay for your degree and the visit to the planetarium. That goal should take precedent.

Fancy A Marshmallow? Or Two?

Resisting temptations and exercising self-control are perhaps the most overlooked aspects of improving willpower. When you do not exercise self-control, you are losing focus on the bigger picture. Psychologist Walter Mischel conducted a now-famous experiment to test the self-control of children. One-by-one, a child was called into a room and shown a marshmallow on a table. They were told that the researcher would leave the room and they either had the option of eating the marshmallow or waiting for 15 minutes until the researcher returned. If they did, they would receive not one but two marshmallows.

For decades, the researchers tracked how these children fared in life. It turned out that the ones who waited for 15 minutes to get 2 marshmallows, meaning they were able to delay gratification, had more academic and social success later in life.

Take a moment and reflect on this situation. As a child, what decision would you make? Did you have the willpower to wait for 15 minutes? Were you able to see the bigger picture? What about now as an adult? Have the results changed or are they the same?

Now, I am positive your goals are sure to have moved beyond the acquisition of marshmallows. But do you focus on the bigger picture? Do you focus on the trade-offs? To find success in life, one must understand the trade-offs and figure out what can be sacrificed for a greater reward. Consider these questions when evaluating your decisions:

- What will happen if you choose Option A? What will happen if you choose Option B?
- What are the pros and cons of Option A?
- What are the pros and cons of Option B?

While you may not have the time or need for evaluating each and every decision, if you practice the above method when making big decisions, it will improve your willpower – and in the long run, help you develop strong focus.

Action Steps

Now you understand that willpower isn't as complicated to exercise as you thought it might be. But it is crucial.

Before we head on to the next chapter, make sure you take these action steps:

- Write down your long-term goals and prioritize them.
- Write down your urgent tasks and prioritize them.
- Reflect on if you feel your willpower has improved or gotten worse in the last year.
- Write down three big upcoming decisions you have to make.
- Write and analyze the trade-offs with these decisions.

In the next chapter, you will learn about the necessity of forming good habits – and the dangers of bad habits!

Chapter Six: How to Create Powerful Habits

"Watch your thoughts for they become words. Watch your words for they become actions. Watch your actions for they become...habits. Watch your habits, for they become your character. And watch your character, for it becomes your destiny! What we think we become." – **Margaret Thatcher**

In this chapter, you will learn how to bring all the lessons together and turn them into habits.

It's A Habitual Thing

We all have habits, good and bad. When it comes to focus, there are habits to develop strong focus, and habits that cause an immense lack of focus. By now you have learned how to use focus to improve certain aspects of your life. You have also learned about how a lack of focus hinders your performance in these aspects of life. Pay attention now to what habits to maintain, and what habits to eradicate to ensure your focus remains strong.

Good Habits

Here are the good habits:

Be an active audience member as opposed to a passive one. What does this mean? I encouraged reading in Chapter Two because this is an active pursuit and forces you to focus on the text. But what about listening to music or watching a film or television show? These are passive forms of entertainment and do not require the focus that reading does. So, when you engage in a passive form of entertainment, you must convert them into active forms of entertainment in order to develop strong focus. Avoid having the television running in the background when you are working. Similarly, when you are watching television, your attention should be on the film or show and not on working or answering your phone. With music, we often tend to play it in the background. While this is not inherently harmful, can you recall if you ever listen to music actively? Do you know the lyrics of the songs you listen to? Can you provide a summary of the film or television show you watch? Focus on being an active audience member, not a passive one.

Have a realistic, smaller goal in lieu of a larger goal. I have written a lot about goals and looking at the bigger picture. Each undertaking may have smaller goals within it which you can "check-off" as you go. If you get into the habit of approaching your tasks in this manner, you will have an easier time focusing on the bigger picture. Conversely, if you only look at each task as a behemoth venture, it may cause you to be discouraged and lose your focus.

Using a checklist is highly recommended in such a situation. Here is how you can break it down. I will use the example of writing a book:

- Conduct research on the topic.
- Develop an outline of the different chapters and sections in the book and what is to be included in them.
- Write an introduction.
- Write one full chapter per day.
- After writing, allot a few days to edit the book.
- Take a break and come back to the book to revise it.

If you approach your project in steps such as in this example, it will help you maintain your focus. If you simply think "I have to write a book," the apprehension may cause you to lose focus.

You do not put off the annoying chores! I have already discussed procrastination and the dangers of putting things off. One aspect of our lives which we tend to procrastinate on the most are the chores which cause us the most inconvenience or even annoyance. Whether it is filing our taxes, taking out the trash, preparing our meals, or washing the dishes, when prioritizing your tasks, these smaller tasks should come first. After you have finished your breakfast, the next step is to begin your homework, correct? Wrong! You must wash your dishes immediately – despite your natural tendency being to allow the dishes to pile up and attending to them at a later stage. Use this approach for all of the smaller tasks.

You don't just "go with the flow." Hear me out. This may work for you and, like multitasking, it is not inherently a bad thing. However, this book is intended for you to develop strong focus. Scheduling your time will help you get a clear picture of what tasks to prioritize – thus improving your focus. Add time durations to your prioritized task list.

Here is an example of the necessary tasks for the day, in no particular order:

- Go for a run.
- Write report for science class (due by end of the day).
- Complete balance sheet for client (due in five days).
- Prepare tax return.
- Treat significant other to dinner.
- Purchase new frying pan.
- Pick up child from school (Must be picked up at 3 PM).

Now what would be the appropriate order of these tasks with the highest priority at the top and the lowest at the bottom? How about this:

- Go for run (This prepares you and gives you energy for the day).
- Prepare tax return (This has an immediate deadline).

- Pick up child from school.
- Complete balance sheet for client.
- Write report for science class.
- Treat significant other to dinner.

Now that you have prioritized your tasks, create a calendar-style schedule and assign timings:

- Go for run. (7 AM – 8 AM).
- Prepare tax return (9:30 – 2 PM).
- Pick up child from school (3 PM).
- Complete balance sheet for client (3:30 PM – 6 PM).
- Write report for science class (6 PM – 7 PM). As this is due in five days, completing a portion is sufficient.
- Treat significant other to dinner (8 PM).

Scheduling is not the most fun aspect of managing one's time, but it is of the utmost importance in developing strong focus. If you are particularly stringent with the timings you impose on yourself, you will automatically focus on the task at hand. Even if you do not necessarily have to complete a task within a particular timeframe or by a particular deadline, you will focus on it if you train your mind to believe that this imposition is crucial.

Bad Habits

And now, here are the bad habits:

You do not have a balanced life! I know you are reading this book to improve your focus for life success. But life success does not only relate to work. The social aspect of life also needs focus. There must be an equal amount of focus when you are spending time with your friends as when you are working on an assignment for your job.

Take a pause and grab your notebook. At the end of each week, record how much time is spent on the following activities:

- Chores – Household chores, errands, the necessities of life.
- Professional and/or academic work – How much time do you spend working or doing your homework for school?
- Leisure – How much time are you spending enjoying yourself? Hanging out with friends and family, watching television, etc.
- Free time – How much time of yours is free and has nothing scheduled? Are there any times during your week which you have nothing planned and nothing that requires your immediate attention? The goal should be to have at least a few hours per week of free time, which you are allowed to spend as you please, guilt-free!

Begin each week by looking back at how you divided your time. There will probably not be an equal distribution between these four activities, but you should ensure that they are close. Are you working 80% of the time and have no time to complete your necessary chores? And do you go weeks without finding time for leisure?

You do not prioritize your activities. Neglecting prioritization is a bad habit which will cause you to lose focus. You have seen examples of how to create a list of priorities; now you will see what happens when those priorities are in an order that leaves much to be desired! Here is an example:

- Go out to dinner.
- Study for exam.
- Go watch a movie.
- Purchase groceries.
- Finish project for work.

You remember our friend Bob? To properly illustrate the danger of poor prioritization, let's see what happens if Bob uses this example. Bob has an urgent project for work which needs completing. He also has to study for a particularly difficult exam, which he will take in a few days. Yet his main priority seems to be going out with his friends for dinner, and later going to watch a movie. His focus on his exam and his project for work will certainly diminish. Purchasing groceries is a necessary chore and should be taken just as seriously.

Take a look at a typical day – do you prioritize the less urgent or less important tasks first? Do you relax the entire day and spend the last few hours doing the important work, before dozing off? Bad prioritizing will cause a lack of focus.

Of course, there are more bad habits and they are often the opposite of the good habits! You have read about the actions to take to develop strong focus. Ensure that your focus is not harmed by doing the opposite of these actions: if you do not prioritize, do not schedule, do not exercise your mind, you will lose focus.

Action Steps

Now that you know what habits to partake in, take these action steps recap:

- Write down any bad habits you have which are harming your focus. Leave a large chunk of space between each bad habit.
- Within the white space, write the antidote for this bad habit. Use a different color ink than the color used for the bad habit. Perhaps in red ink you can write "I procrastinate often." and in blue ink you can write "I will prioritize and schedule my tasks."
- As you work toward eliminating these bad habits, cross them off when you feel you have overcome them!

Final Words

Let's revisit our friend Bob one more time. Bob seems to live a life without focus. What's a little procrastination here and there? Does he really need to carry a planner and schedule each day? Is there really an issue with biting off more than he can chew? If you are in Bob's shoes, you know that this is not the approach you should take. This lack of focus leads to less productivity, a poor work ethic, and a mismanagement of your time. This will guarantee very little in life, except that you (and Bob!) will not find the success you wish to attain.

Everyone's life is hectic, but you now have an advantage: **You *now* know how to focus**.

Refer to this book whenever you are having any difficulty focusing, or in any aspect of focus. Whether you need to fuel your productivity, find motivation, build self-discipline, or improve willpower, this book will be there to help you with those. And if you want to deepen your understanding even more, check out the 'Resources' section.

You now know that focus extends beyond putting the phone away while driving or figuring out how to not fall asleep during a monotonous speech by a teacher or a colleague at a meeting. Focus is what gives you an *edge* over others in finding success, in both the professional and personal aspects of your life.

I would like to thank you for reading this book. This book was intended to be written as a practical guide for engaging in activities to develop strong focus and to demonstrate how a strong focus in turn improves your performance in life activities. If I could ask you a favor, it would be for you to pass this book on to at least one person whom you believe may benefit from it. I wish to help more individuals find success in their lives by developing strong focus.

And one more thing! This one's for you. Look back at the first page of your notebook. Reflect on what you wrote. Re-read your mission statement and your viewpoints on your quality of focus. Take a few minutes and rewrite this viewpoint. If you followed the steps outlined in the book, this should have improved.

Do not worry if there are still issues – developing strong focus does not happen overnight, and it is a continuous process. You may still procrastinate or may still be tempted to devour the marshmallow immediately. However, by continuously practicing these methods, you will develop laser-sharp focus!

Don't let any setbacks hinder your progress; look at the bigger picture. Think of what you will achieve by continuing to develop your focus!

Resources

Books

- *Hyper Focus: How To Be More Productive in a World of Distraction* – Chris Bailey
- *Deep Work: Rules for Focused Success in a Distracted World* – Cal Newport
- *Willpower Doesn't Work: Discover the Hidden Keys to Success* – Benjamin Hardy
- *Accelerated Learning: How to Learn Fast With Ease* – Kevin Garnett
- *The Art of Learning: An Inner Journey to Optimal Performance* – Joshua Waitzkin
- *The Willpower Instinct: How Self-Control Works, Why It Matters, and What You Can Do To Get More of it* – Kelly McGonigal

Websites

- Jamesclear.com
- Zenhabits.net
- Lifehacker.com
- Scotthyoung.com
- Collegeinfogeek.com
- Benjaminhardy.com

Podcasts

- The Tim Ferriss Show
- Master of Scale
- The Productivity Podcast
- The Mission Daily
- Achieve Your Goals

BONUS CHAPTER: What is Accelerated Learning?

Below, you will find a free bonus chapter from my book **'Accelerated Learning**: *How to Learn Fast With Ease.'*

Enjoy!

It is my way of saying thanks for

- reading this book, and
- taking <u>focused</u> action. You rock!

Let's get started, shall we?

***

The problem from which you, I, and pretty much everybody else suffers is that education, whether for school, the workplace, or life in general, has shaped us. It has created prejudices, used largely unsuccessful methodology, and damaged the self-esteem of many. It has made us think of failure as a disaster. It has created the impression that we should get everything right – what are we learning if we can do it already? – and that to make mistakes or go through a learning process is somehow a bad thing. It has handicapped us with what Carol Dweck calls a 'fixed mindset.'

Accelerated learning is a way to overcome this. The concept of accelerated learning, sometimes simply called AL, is not a new one. However, its freshness of approach and its challenge to the traditional ways in which we learn new concepts and ideas makes it still a novel way to improve yourself.

In this chapter, we will look at some of the guiding principles behind accelerated learning, which come together to enable people to improve their understanding, problem solving, and acquisition of knowledge with remarkable effectiveness. The principles should be viewed rather like a recipe. Every element small or large plays an important role. Create the dish with just one ingredient missing and, while it won't kill you or send you rushing to the hospital with an acute case of food poisoning, it won't taste very good. Like a good cake, accelerated learning is all or nothing.

The Basic Principles

Underpinning the idea of accelerated learning are some basic, guiding principles.

Firstly, AL uses the idea of **exploiting and enhancing the ways in which people naturally learn**. This means that the system works as well with the four-year-old encountering letters for the first time as the eighty-year-old joining the University of Life and acquiring new skills for their later years.

The second underlying principle is that **accelerated learning seeks to break into the aspects of our potential which are often left undisturbed**, and therefore unused, by traditional teaching methods. It is common sense, if we think about it, that the more of our capabilities that are engaged by learning, the better we will learn. Therefore, this learning technique takes advantage of the numerous latent talents humans possess. It calls on the physical, creative, musical, artistic, visual, kinetic and emotional aspects of mankind, utilizing all of these in the development of the mind's learning capabilities.

Holistic Approach

Accelerated learning can best be described as a holistic approach to learning. As you head through this book you will come across tips to help you become an expert in this field. But, in a way, offering separate techniques is a little artificial. To become a proper, accelerated learner, you must apply the entire philosophy, rather than pick and choose only some of its elements.

This book will consider the following in more detail in later chapters, but accelerated learning makes sound assumptions about the way we learn and the environment which best enhances this.

- **The way we learn involves all of us**. For example, our brain processes information from each of the senses. Therefore, to maximize learning, we need to create the situation whereby the learner, be it ourselves or others, touches, smells, tastes, sees, and hears information.

- **Learners need to see their acquisition as creativity rather than consumption**. In traditional learning methods, the recipient is fed information or skills which they attempt to acquire. There are two fundamental failings with this approach. Firstly, learning is automatically limited by the range of the teaching material. Secondly, the brain is less effective at absorbing information than it is it at creating skills or knowledge, probably largely because being fed details is pretty boring, while being active and creative is more interesting.

- **Collaboration is a better way to learn than competition.** Of course, this is a concept which challenges the very heart of education, whether in the workplace, home, or educational institution. Examinations are competitive. Promotion at work is competitive. If we trace it back, we can see the reasons for this. Those expectations of a competitive environment are the product of people who were both themselves competitive and also successful in that competition. People recreate their own image. Yet it takes little thought to realize that competitive learning only suits those who are firstly competitive by their nature and secondly, successful at such competition. For the majority of people, in all walks of life, who simply are unmotivated by fighting against their peers, a competitive learning environment is one that is anathema to their naturally collaborative personalities.

- **People respond best to a variety of learning styles**. There can be a tendency on the part of the educator to attempt to replicate their own favored learning style as they impart their knowledge. As such, many people fail to be engaged as they are confronted with a style which counters their own.

- **When people learn, they do so on many different levels**. They can see things literally, metaphorically, intuitively, and so forth. They can acquire both practical skills and cognitive methods to problem solving; each has their place and is equally worthwhile. To illustrate the point with an example, in the traditional education system, cognitive abilities are frequently accorded higher status than practical ones, yet each plays their important role.

- **Learning is doing**. That is a key principle behind the theory of accelerated learning. It picks up on an earlier idea that when people are active, their ability to learn improves.

- **The brain is able to absorb information given in images instantly.**

- **The brain works better in a positive environment**. That does not mean, as is often interpreted, that everything in the environment is perfect, but more it means creating an environment in which learners, whatever their age of level, are confident and secure enough to feel able to test, experiment and, on occasion, fail. It is the ability to learn from that failure that encourages really deep and effective learning.

Next, we will look at the educational and social theory behind accelerated learning and discover a little of the history and context that underpins it.

***

This is the end of this bonus chapter.

Want to continue reading?

Then get your copy of "Accelerated Learning" at your favorite bookstore!

Did You Like This Book?

If you enjoyed this book, I would like to ask you for a favor. Would you be kind enough to share your thoughts and post a review of this book? Just a few sentences would already be really helpful.

Your voice is important for this book to reach as many people as possible.

The more reviews this book gets, the more people will be able to find it and also learn how they can develop Super Focus.

***

IF YOU DID NOT LIKE THIS BOOK, THEN PLEASE TELL ME!

You can email me at **feedback@semsoli.com**, to share with me what you did not like.

Perhaps I can change it.

A book does not have to be stagnant, in today's world. With feedback from readers like yourself, I can improve the book. So, you can impact the quality of this book, and I welcome your feedback. Help make this book better for everyone!

Thank you again for reading this book and good luck with applying everything you have learned!

I'm rooting for you...

Brain Teaser Answers

These are the answers to the brain teasers in Chapter Two:

Brain Teaser 1: ONE WORD.

Brain Teaser 2: The letter 'M'.

Brain Teaser 3: A river.

Brain Teaser 4: add the letter 'S'.

By The Same Author

DECLUTTER YOUR LIFE

The Art of Tidying Up, Organizing Your Home, Decluttering Your Mind, & Minimalist Living
(Less is More!)

KEVIN GARNETT

Notess

www.ingramcontent.com/pod-product-compliance
Lightning Source LLC
Chambersburg PA
CBHW072041110526
44592CB00012B/1511